STEAM MEMORIES: 1950's - 1960's
No. 72: LMS PATRIOTS
NORMAN PREEDY

Copyright Book Law Publications 2014
ISBN 978-1-909625-34-1

INTRODUCTION

Featuring the ex-LMS 'Patriots' this album basically deals with two classes of locomotives – 6P and 7P 4-6-0s. The latter were the LMS/BR rebuilds which brought eighteen members of the original 52 engines up to 7P standard in line with the 'Royal Scots.' The original engines remained virtually as built but with some extra safety features added by British Railways. The last of the parallel boiler express passenger engines, the 'Pats' would do most things entrusted to them, with reliability being at the forefront.

Many of them never reached their thirtieth birthdays – though only by months in most cases – simply because they were working their twilight years during the age of motive power transition on BR. However, their owners certainly got their mon'ey's-worth' worth, and more, out of the class.

The assembled illustrations will hopefully present a broad insight into the operations of the class during BR's steam decades, and along with relevant captions we include a number of images featuring the nameplates carried by the named members of this glorious class.

David Allen, Newstead, September 2014.

(Cover) No.45506 THE ROYAL PIONEER CORPS at Kettering.

(previous page) 'Patriot' No.45551, one of the un-named members of the class, picks-up from Dillicar troughs whilst working an Up fitted freight in 1951.

Printed and bound by The Amadeus Press, Cleckheaton, West Yorkshire
First published in the United Kingdom by Book Law Publications, 382 Carlton Hill, Nottingham, NG4 1JA

Class leader No.45500 **PATRIOT** runs onto the Crewe North turntable on 3rd July 1954. The less than immaculate 6P was allocated to Longsight at this time but would be transferring to Upperby by the end of the year. Most, but not all, of the 'Patriots' were allocated to Crewe North at one time or another. Three of them never did time at 5A: No.45520, 45527, and 45538. Three others managed just weeks: 45500, 45536, and 45550. All the rest put in varying terms from months to years, some doing multiple residencies. Our subject was allocated from 20th February to 10th April 1937.

(right) No.5500 (No.5971 up to May 1934) carried the name **CROXTETH** until 25th February 1937 when it was renamed PATRIOT. This is one of the plates originally carried by 'Claughton' No.5964 (No.1914 up to June 1926) before that engine was scrapped in 1934 and the plates became museum pieces for that short time prior to No.5500 acquiring them.

3

No.45501 at Crewe works in circa 1954 coaled-up and ready to leave the shops for some running-in. The low winter sun shows that it is about midday and the amount of frost on the ground along with a smattering of snow has prompted the use of braziers, which always looked so inviting! This was a Longsight engine at the time of the photograph – it served 9A for one year and nine days, in one stint!

Approximately seven years later, on 7th August 1961, and No.45501 is looking just the opposite to its external appearance in the previous illustration. Now a resident of Upperby (via the likes of Carnforth, Mold Junction, and Warrington!), where this scene was captured, and up-to-date on the equipment front, with ATC and electrification flashes, the 6P has less than three weeks in traffic before being condemned. Note the size of the wheel bosses on both 45501 and 45500 - they were the original 'Claughton' wheels.

ST DUNSTAN'S – the name carried by No.5501 from 1937. The earlier appellation, **SIR FRANK REE**, went to sister No.5530.

(above) About nine miles from Shap, No.45503 THE ROYAL LEICESTERSHIRE REGIMENT starts to dig into the climb at Clifton & Lowther with an Up express. We have no date but the 'Patriot' has been equipped with ATC and carries the full complement of electrification warning flashes so it must be very early Sixties' because the 6P was withdrawn in August 1961. Perhaps this was one of its last outings before being condemned. *(below)* No.45503 working a fitted freight – 1st August 1953.

No.45503 was a Carnforth engine for two months and twenty-two days during the summer of 1960 and here at Ravengless, on Sunday 4th September 1960, during its final week at 24L, the 4-6-0 looks rather smart and has been cleaned up for this special working; the front end seems to have received a lick of paint too. A considerable amount of attention is being lavished on the engine by the assembled crowd, and rightly so because clean engines were becoming quite rare on BR during that time.

The 1938 version of the nameplate, as carried by No.5503. This unit had been active since 1688 as a regiment of foot and was known simply by the names of its current Colonel. From 1751 it was known as the 17th Regiment of Foot. From 1782 it became the 17th (Leicestershire) Regiment of Foot. At its height during the First World War, the Regiment consisted nineteen battalions! Approximately 6,000 men from the regiment lost their lives during those four years of conflict.

The 1948 version of the nameplate which unusually has been shaped around the text rather than being a curved block as previously. The 'Royal' status was granted to the regiment in 1946. Amalgamated into the newly formed Royal Anglian Regiment from September 1964, the RLR – like so many others – no longer exists as a unit of the British Army.

7

Allocated away from the old Western Division at Upperby to Bristol Barrow Road shed on the former Midland Division from November 1958, No.45504 **ROYAL SIGNALS** never did receive ATC but it got to a number of places where it had probably not previously visited. One such place was York and on 23rd May 1959 it was photographed passing through Pontefract with a York-Bristol express, a duty which it took up regularly, and with ease.

Sans 82E shed plate latterly, No.45504 went about its work with a certain mystery as to where it belonged. This is Derby in the summer of 1962 when the 6P was in charge of a southbound express comprising ten vehicles. It has steam to spare as it crosses the River Derwent bridge whilst slowing for the station stop. This would be the 'Patriot's' last year on these or any other workings.

The **ROYAL SIGNALS** nameplate and regimental badge, the latter featuring Mercury. The actual title of the regiment is the Royal Corps of Signals. Formed in 1920 under a Royal Warrant signed by the then Secretary of State for War, Winston Churchill, the corps has origins going back to 1870 when the first telegraph signallers were formed into a troop of the Royal Engineers.

Upperby's No.45505 **THE ROYAL ARMY ORDNANCE CORPS** stands alongside the ash plant as Newton Heath shed during servicing on 21st October 1961. The tender is already full after a visit to the coaler – note that the tender (No.4569) is one of the 3,500 gallon high straight-sided examples of which three were 'pooled' to the class; Nos.4570 and 4573 were the others which were coupled to various engines as follows: No.4573 to No.45515 from 10th January 1957 to 9th February 1957. No.4570 to No.45515 from 17th August 1957 to 15th March 1958. No.4573 to No.45539 from 1st May 1956 to 10th January 1957. No.4573 to No.45550 from 29th December 1942 to 23rd January 1956. No.4570 to No.45551 from 2nd May 1958 to withdrawal. No.4569 was coupled to No.45505 from 2nd April 1960 to withdrawal. None of the ten high-sided tenders (Nos.4564-4573) were built specifically for the 'Patriots' but for 'Jubilees' Nos.5607 to 5616 in 1934.

On a Sunday in April 1959 No.45505 had charge of a London (Euston)-Manchester (London Road) express and was photographed passing through Northwich station whilst diversions were in force to keep traffic away from the Manchester-Crewe line south of Stockport, whilst electrification and station rebuilding work was being undertaken. This engine's stint at Longsight started in September 1954 and ended in September 1960 when Upperby got it yet again – for the 4th time since 1947 – 9A, which had the 'Patriot' just the once, had gained it from Preston, a shed which was home to No.45505 (and others) three times!

THE ROYAL ARMY ORDNANCE CORPS nameplate and crest in all its glory. Fitted in 1947, nearly thirty years after Royal was added to the title of the corps, on amalgamation of the Army Ordnance Corps and Army Ordnance Department. Responsible for supply of munitions and weaponry. The common translation of the Latin is 'To the Warrior his Arms' whereas the literal one is 'His Missiles to the one who is Thundering.' The RAOC was amalgamated in April 1993 with others to become part of the Royal Logistics Corps.

There is no such thing as safety in numbers! En route to oblivion! Both statements carry weight for this illustration which features Nos.45506 **THE ROYAL PIONEER CORPS** and 45504 **ROYAL SIGNALS** travelling north through Stafford on their way to Crewe for works attention. The date (to the day) is uncertain but the pair had left their home shed at Barrow Road in Bristol and travelled via the former Midland route to Birmingham and then onwards to Crewe – a bit of thought about the route has kept the engines running smokebox leading, throughout. Both engines are in steam and complete in every respect, nameplates, numberplates and shedplates all in place; the driver of No.45504 even appears to be wearing a beret with a Royal Signals cap badge, perhaps in honour of the event which will unfold when the two 6Ps arrive at Crewe. Of course there are many clues here already: the inclement, probably freezing, weather with a threatening overcast sky (more of a mood and scene setter than a clue perhaps), and the year – 1962 – the year of the great purge on steam locomotives when twenty-five, more than half, of the surviving 'Patriots' were condemned. Our pair would be received at Crewe South shed where fires would be dropped, boilers and tenders emptied, and then temporary storage in the works reception sidings with countless others which were there for repair, overhaul or scrapping; for these two it was the latter. During week ending Saturday 17th March 1962 they were both condemned and shortly afterwards cut up. The cutting up shop at Crewe was sometimes so efficient and clinical that they often broke up engines before the withdrawal w.e. dates! The date of this photograph therefore must have been around the end of February or perhaps the beginning of March 1962 because Crewe didn't hang around when it came to dismantling locomotives. As an aside, note the foundations for the overhead catenary awaiting the stanchions. The exact location chosen by the photographer was at the junction of the line to Wellington, just north of the station.

Happier days – when a visit to the works at Crewe meant a new coat of paint to finish off a complete overhaul. Such was the case here for No.45506, or was it? The image is undated but a couple of known clues, the electrification warning flash on the firebox casing, and the BR crest on the tender, lead us to about 1960 or 1961. The stabling of the Tram Engine on the adjacent road would be a known quantity to some people, as would the large piece of electrical apparatus sitting astride the road on the other side of the 6P but this compiler is uncertain of both of those items (the presence of the electrical equipment is a mystery in itself!). However, getting back to known facts, the 9A shedplate! The last time this engine was allocated to Longsight was in early 1947 and assuming we have the approximate date for this illustration being recorded, the 'Patriot' was then part of the Bristol Barrow Road fleet. So, what is afoot? Has someone put the wrong plate on after the repair? It certainly looks that way and it wasn't unknown at Crewe. The engine was in 'shops' from late October 1960 to late January 1961 receiving a Casual Light repair which would tie up nicely with this illustration. Note the staining and spillage on the plating below the smokebox door; this may well be the residue from concrete which had been poured, via hand-held buckets, into the bottom of the smokebox to help make it airtight. The 'temporary fix' was used at many of the depots associated with this class, unofficially at first but as time went by it appears that the method was given credence at Crewe too. I might however be wrong but it certainly looks like cement staining!

5507 - We don't have an illustration of the locomotive but we have secured this image of one of the nameplates (left-hand side) attached to the engine. The motto seems straightforward enough. When No.5507 was named in 1937, a ceremony was held to mark the occasion.

Every class had an 'odd-one-out' and the 'Patriots' latterly had No.45508 with that terrible chimney. Un-named, our subject acquired the chimney in 1956 as part of an experimental draughting system which was not repeated with any other members of the class; was it a success or failure, we shall never know the truth. No.45508 (3rd December 1960) was the second engine to be condemned after No.45502 (3rd September 1960); they were the only ones to succumb that year. We are at Tebay, circa 1960, and No.45508 has charge of an Up freight. The smokebox door has taken a hammering and perhaps the eventual distortion added some weight to the case for withdrawal!? Now then, that first vehicle looks very continental whilst the second vehicle looks equally unfamiliar.

(above) The desolation of winter can make most things dull and limp but steam has a mind of its own and seems to thrive in the cold air. Such is the case at Tuffley near Gloucester in 1953 as No.45509 **THE DERBYSHIRE YEOMANRY** runs south with an eight-coach express for Bristol. This 'Patriot' had only carried a name since November 1951 and was the last-but-one of the class to be named. At the time of the photograph No.45509 was a Derby engine having transferred from the WCML at Crewe North in October 1951. The 6P would work the Midland lines from Derby for another seven years before a final transfer took it to Newton Heath. This broad stretch of railway south of Gloucester is now reduced to an Up and a Down track. *(below)* **TDY** with a northbound, Up working at Gloucester (Eastgate) during the engine's seven year stint on the Bristol–York road. Being based at Derby, and taking up residence at 26A for its final three years of life, No.45509 was never fitted with ATC.

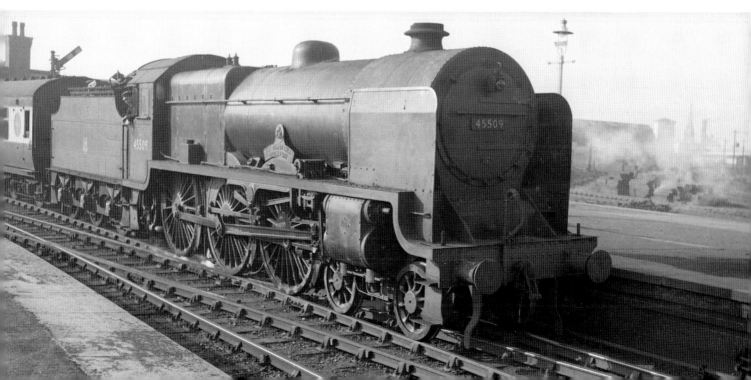

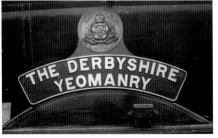

No.45509 at its final abode, Newton Heath shed in September 1958. From here the 6P would work westwards to the seaside at Blackpool, Fleetwood, or Southport and probably Liverpool; LMS divisional demarkation lines were mainly still in place even ten years after BR came into being. To the east, trips to Wakefield, Leeds, Bradford and perhaps Hull beckoned but it was to be a short-lived existence at 26A because No.45509 was withdrawn during the week ending Saturday 12th August 1961, Crewe again doing the necessary demolition. 1961 was a bad year for the original engines of the class, with nine of them being condemned; the first two had gone in September and December 1960, not quite reaching the 30-years revenue earning goal of their makers, the LMS.

TDY plate and badge.

Willesden's No.45510 runs towards the south end of Crewe station on Sunday 6th July 1958 to await a southbound working. Somehow, the un-named 'Patriots' brought a tinge of disappointment to most train-spotters when they ran past; 45510 would have done so firstly on North shed during the morning, and in the station during this glorious early afternoon. Working mainly on the WCML, this engine has been fitted with ATC which virtually ensured its continued employment from depots located along the main line. However, ATC did not ensure continued employment and our subject was withdrawn from Lancaster Green Ayre shed during w.e. 9th June 1962. The Crewe North 'Scot' trying to hide its identity on the left was No.46161 **KING'S OWN**, recently out of works after a Heavy General and was now ready for the 'off' with an Up working.

Long-time Willesden resident No.45511 **ISLE OF MAN** blows-off alongside 1A's coaler on Saturday 29th August 1959. This view shows off the Fowler 3,500 gallon tender for what it was, small. Holding just five and a half tons of coal, as this one is, the whole thing appeared top-heavy. What made the tenders appear even 'dinkier' were the 1st and 2nd BR badges, the emblem, and then the crest; this one appears smaller than that worn by the 'Jinty' located beneath the coaler. The tender coupled to 45511 here was its fourth example of the type, No.3933; it would acquire a fifth in September 1960. However, before then our 6P would be transferred away from London to a place which was to become one of the final outposts of BR steam – Carnforth on 17th October 1959. In 1960 it served Mold Junction, Warrington Dallam and Carlisle Upperby, in that order, but its services were not required for long at either place. Inevitably withdrawal took place during the week ending 11th February 1961, breaking-up followed shortly afterwards. The unrebuilt Patriots did appear to be wiped-out fairly quickly and once into the works at Crewe they soon became history.

18 The original nameplate from 1938 without the coat of arms.   Transformation after the granting.

Upperby's No.45512 stops alongside the water column on the Down fast at Stafford station at some time in the Fifties'. Without an actual date we cannot be more precise than that because **BUNSEN** was resident at the Carlisle depot from 28th May 1949 until withdrawal in March 1965. Anyway, was it simply water which the 7P required or was something amiss at the front end? The latter looks distinctly possible especially with the nearest cylinder. Rebuilt in July 1948, No.45512 was one of nine converted from 6P to 7P (at first they were 5X to 6P) during that year; six were done in 1947, two in 1946, and the final one – 45522 – in February 1949. Stafford station's infrastructure is still very much intact but sections of the roof have already been removed in anticipation of the rebuilding which would coincide with electrification of the WCML.

20　Looking a bit healthier, though just as dirty, No.45512 at Shap Wells on Friday 3rd July 1959 with eleven on!

Now that is a long train by any standards. This is Crewe North's No.45513 at Scout Green on Shap and luckily the 6P is coasting down hill on a glorious evening during the summer of 1954. The engine remained nameless throughout its life but in 1943 it was chosen to carry the name Sir W.A.STANIER. As things turned out it never happened and we all know that the famous name ended up in a much more appropriate location! In the meantime, just look at this lot which features numerous vans, 4-wheel, 6-wheel and bogie, a milk tank, and continental vans of varying origins and designs. We are assuming that the train is mainly empty and lets hope those connections are all tight and secure.

With notebook in hand, a lone spotter observes No.45513's southbound progress from what appears to be a favourite location for the local enthusiasts.
22 The date is unrecorded but the 'Patriot' looks to be in bad condition at the front end, and has yet to acquire ATC.

Traversing the Up fast through Heaton Norris junction in 1955, Camden's No.45514 **HOLYHEAD** looks resplendent at the head of an afternoon Manchester (London Road)-London (Euston) express. The first stop for this train, at Stockport (Edgeley), is but a couple of minutes away and the regulator will soon be eased off. Rebuilt in March 1947 as No.5514, this 'Patriot' was allocated to Edge Hill at the time of conversion but shortly after leaving works, it was transferred to Holyhead, the first of nine such transfers which saw the engine go to Bushbury, Crewe North, Upperby, Camden, and eventually Derby although that final re-allocation probably never happened because the engine was withdrawn during the week of transfer – 27th May 1961 – the first of the rebuilt engines to go! The junction here was controlled by Heaton Norris Junction box (obscured in the steam and left of the train) which had recently been replaced as part of the Stockport to Levenshulme colour-light re-signalling, the base of the old box is still visible alongside the fourth carriage. Note the point rodding which wasn't renewed but extended into the new box which required 125 levers!

(above) No.45515 **CAERNARVON** spent most of its BR career working from Edge Hill shed – 19th November 1949 to 2nd April 1960 – and in this undated illustration the 4-6-0 is undergoing examination after servicing at its home shed. Neither ATC nor warning flashes have been fitted so we are looking at the late 1950s, or perhaps earlier; the crest/emblem being hidden by dirt doesn't help either. Amongst the various sheds served by the class early on in their careers, this 'Patriot' can add Aston and Shrewsbury to its tally. *(below)* Although Carlisle Upperby was home to many of the class, including No.45515 on a number of occasions, when this image was recorded at the north end of Citadel station on 29th July 1961 the 6P was a Newton Heath engine. It appears that 26A had no more inclination to cleaning its charges than any other shed during this period. Earlier it was mentioned that during their final years, the unrebuilt 'Patriots' had to have radical but innovative, and unofficial, treatment to temporarily cure the holes developing in the bottom of the smokeboxes – fill the void with concrete or a strong cement mix! This engine has the tell-tale stains beneath the smokebox door showing that it was a practice at most depots. It worked! ATC and warning flashes are now accepted 'extras' on the WCML.

(above) Bank Hall's No.45517 stables at, apparently, Trafford Park awaiting a westbound working. It was unusual to find 27A engines of any type at the former Cheshire Lines depot so this must have been quite a surprise for the photographer. No.45517 reached the former L&Y depot at Liverpool on transfer from Willesden at the end of July 1958; a lifetime on the old Western Division saw the 4-6-0 working for a different crowd on the former Central Division but note the ATC which would not now be required. This engine's usual lot at Bank Hall was working the Liverpool (Exchange)–Newcastle (Central) – via the ex-L&Y route – as far as York from where it would wait for a return working back to Exchange; the 6P continued on those jobs until early 1962. Withdrawn in early June, she was broken up at Crewe. Note the wrong-facing BR crest adorning the tender; they got it wrong even on the small size transfers! *(below)* Getting No.45517 ready for its return journey from York to Liverpool circa 1961. *K.R.Pirt.*

Coasting down Shap, No.45518 **BRADSHAW,** on lowly duties, at Scout Green on a gloriously clear 23rd March 1960. The 6P had just notched another 'unusual' shed to its tally – Warrington Dallam – as it was passed around the Region like a hot potato! Aston was next in line, then Edge Hill and finally Lancaster Green Ayre. Note the livestock wagons with real cattle aboard (*see also* No.45503 at Penrith in 1953)!

One of the **BRADSHAW** nameplates in preservation, along with a worksplate from the 1933 (re)building date.

An atrocious looking No.45519 **LADY GODIVA** runs north through Tuffley in the summer of 1961 with a fitted freight. Resident at Barrow Road since November 1958, the 6P was condemned in March 1962, following Nos.45504 and 45506 to Crewe for breaking up. All three of the 82E 'Patriots' were transferred from Upperby to Bristol on 15th November 1958, for jobs such as this, and working the Midland route express passenger trains to Birmingham and beyond alongside Barrow Road's 'Jubilees' 6Ps. Did the 'Lady' make her own way to Crewe for that March 1962 rendezvous with the breaker?

Two views of No.45519's BR period workings *(above)* at York awaiting departure with the York–Bristol circa 1959. The J72 in the middle was a lot younger than the 6P, and not much older than the new Type 4 diesel on the left! *(below)* Immaculate at Birmingham (New Street) in 1957; it appears that the engine has actually been cleaned, where it shows, but the tender has yet to have any attention. At the time **LADY GODIVA** was a Longsight engine – 17th November 1956 to 14th June 1958 – and would have worked from Manchester with this semi-fast via Stoke. No.45519 never did get ATC having left the WCML before it was fitted.

No.45519 at Crewe works in March 1960. Now established at Barrow Road, the 6P will spend the rest of its life at the former Midland depot and to help elongate its operational life somewhat – by another two years anyway – Crewe has managed to pour some concrete into the void at the bottom of the smokebox. It would be interesting to know at what stage of the repair was the concrete actually poured into the smokebox; seemingly after paint has been applied!

29

(above) So that's what they looked like in BR mixed traffic lined black livery – smart! No.45520 **LLANDUDNO** has arrived at Birmingham's New Street station on Tuesday 30th August 1949 straight from the paint shop at Crewe by the looks of it, the little bit of road dirt on the tender having been accumulated en route! However, more to the point is that the Longsight engine has just left the care of the works and was probably on a running-in turn prior to working home. *(below)* Two years later and No.45520 looks no better than any of the class did during their final days. Still in lined mixed traffic black – just discernible on the cabside – the 4-6-0 is working an ordinary passenger train near Poynton on 3rd September 1951. No.45520 only ever worked from four sheds during its lifetime: Kentish Town initially, Edge Hill, Longsight and Preston; the latter for just three months in the summer of 1955. The first of the Derby built batch of 1933, No.45520 was withdrawn from Edge Hill shed in May 1962. Crewe did the scrapping.

Wearing the lined Brunswick green at Shrewsbury in 1956.

The 1937 nameplate prior to the civic enhancement.

Preservation with the civic coat of arms. 31

No.45521 **RHYL** hauling an Up express on the WCML, north of Lichfield circa 1961. ATC and electrification warning flashes are fitted but that coaching stock looks ancient and besides not giving this compiler any clues, it will be giving the passengers therein a 'memorable' ride no doubt. Most probably an Edge Hill engine at this time – it moved to Springs Branch in mid-September 1961 – it was operation until the end of the summer timetable in 1963.

The inscription on the coat of arms is in Welsh rather than Latin. The complete package.

Definitely 12th August 1961! Still an 8A engine, just, No.45521 looks somewhat tired at Carlisle (Citadel) but work beckoned for another couple of years, albeit running from Wigan. Further history in this image is represented by the Express Dairy milk tank in the bay platform behind. Carlisle was a staging point for milk collected from farms ranging out to the west coast on both sides of the border and trains would be marshalled here into trains contained ten or more 6-wheel tanks, and a couple of vans with churns, etc., for the journey south; motive power for the trains ranged from Pacifics to 7P and 6P 4-6-0s.

In the event that we have no illustration of No.45522, we present the nameplate as it was on the locomotive. This plate had no civic badge, nor coat of arms attached! No.45522 was stored at Buxton shed after withdrawal and was then purchased for scrap by Central Wagon Co., Wigan, the only 'Patriot' cut up at that yard but not the only one scrapped in Lancashire as the locomotive works at Horwich took care of a couple of the class.

Upperby shed was still going through the throes of rebuilding when No.45523 **BANGOR** was photographed on the yard on 6th August 1956. A former Carlisle engine, No.45523 was now allocated to Camden (from 7th July 1951) and was coaled-up but not quite ready to return south. Amongst the last of the class to go for scrap (withdrawn w.e. 25th January 1964), our subject transferred to Willesden at the end of January 1961. *David Dalton.*

BLACKPOOL in preservation! This was another plate which had neither badge nor coat-of-arms!

No.45525 **COLWYN BAY** approaches Crewe station with a Down working of *THE MANXMAN* in 1959. Note that ATC is yet to be fitted but more importantly perhaps, there are no electrification warning flashed fitted to the locomotive. However, there is still time for the latter because the overhead was not yet energised and much of system was still to be fitted – note the empty, hanging insulators on some sections of the catenary. The 7P was an Edge Hill steed at this stage of its career but in January 1961 it moved on to Willesden then, in September 1961, it transferred, perhaps appropriately, to Llandudno Junction shed for its final fling before withdrawal in May 1963.

The coat-of-arms attached to Colwyn Bay's nameplate. Once again the Welsh language is preferred for the legend.

(opposite, top) No.45526 **MORECAMBE AND HEYSHAM** works hard through Shap Wells on Tuesday 3rd April 1956 with a twelve-coach Down express. *(opposite, bottom)* On the WCML again but at Dillicar Common with a lightweight Euston–Carlisle express circa 1959. *(above)* The final style of livery worn by the rebuilt engines in the class; dirt and yellow cab stripe! This is No.45526 at Crewe North's shed outlet in August 1964. Withdrawal was just weeks away for the Upperby based engine. *D.H.Beecroft.*

Here is a close-up of the rather smart nameplate!

No.45527 **SOUTHPORT** on No.11 road outside the Paint shop at Crewe in 1956. The tender appears to have been well and truly rubbed down ready for some paint whilst the engine has been cleaned ready for the necessary preparations before the first coats are applied. Note the 'shopping' list on the cab side, with each entry crossed through as completion was attained in the Erecting shop. Allocated to Edge Hill for almost twenty-eight years, No.45527 was one of the longest serving 'Patriots' attached to any depot!

It appears that SOUTHPORT's plate required some t.l.c.

A smart looking No.45529 **STEPHENSON** heads a Liverpool (Lime Street)–London (Euston) express at Crewe in March 1960. The Crewe North 7P has the ATC but is not yet equipped with a 'speedo' but that will come during the next four years this engine had to operate. Note the water column still in situ with all that catenary waiting to be energised! *D.H.Beecroft.*

The 1948 nameplate fitted some time after the rebuilding in 1947. The engine had lost its earlier name in 1937.

We have no date for this view of No.45530 at Low Gill but it appears to be circa 1960. The Up express was probably one of the Anglo-Scottish jobs which has lost its intended motive power – a 'Duchess' or a diesel – and this Camden 7P has been given the job which it would basically swallow. There would be a few disappointed 'spotters' at Crewe and other places perhaps but no one would care what engine was in charge as long as time was kept. I wonder if it was? Meanwhile, savour the Lune valley in all its glory before it was spoilt by the motorway.

With nameplates removed, No.45530 languishes at an unknown location in the mid-1960s with part of the motion also removed. The engine's last recorded shed before 1964 was Willesden to which it transferred in July 1962 but it was later branded with the yellow stripe across the cab denoting that it was not allowed to work on the WCML south of Crewe which basically puts the 1A allocation in the bin and by the end of 1964 it had moved to Kingmoor. It was from there that former **SIR FRANK REE** was withdrawn and sold to a scrapyard in Motherwell at the end of 1965. This image depicts the 4-6-0 at a location near that yard. The diesel shunter was apparently D2441 (the '1' being inconveniently left off the negative) and that was the only one of its class which could have been in the area at the time of the 7Ps arrival in 1966.

A well balanced nameplate?

With a not-quite-completed paint job, No.45531 **SIR FREDERICK HARRISON** stands at the throat of the Paint shop yard at Crewe on Sunday 24th April 1955. This engine was amongst the last of the class to be withdrawn, its final transfer taking it in late 1963 to Springs Branch shed where jobs for steam locomotives were still available.

With seemingly plenty of steam to spare, even though the journey is in the ascension, No.45532 **ILLUSTRIOUS** heads through Chinley South Junction with a Manchester (Central)–London (St Pancras) express on Thursday 28th April 1960. The nine-coach load should have been easy enough for the 7P but the continuous twists and gradients encountered on the main line through the Peak District could be a little bit difficult and having plenty of steam available made life comfortable; the Nottingham based 4-6-0 seems to be coping nicely. It was unusual to find Nottingham based 6P and 7P 'namers' working over the Derby-Manchester line so our subject was probably a stand-in for a steam failure. The production 'Peaks' would not materialise until October 1960 and the ten original 'Peaks' were still, ironically, plying the WCML. However, there was a class of diesel-electrics which were often 'tried' on the London-Manchester expresses during this period – the Metro-Vick Co-Bos! Also, let's not forget the Southern Region built 1-Co-Co-1 diesel-electrics 10201-10203 which saw service on this route during this period. Remember the 'Fell' diesel too but that had been condemned in November 1958. Reader, the choice is yours!

ILLUSTRIOUS again but some months later with electrification warning flashes now affixed to the engine and a semblance of cleaning having taken place around the boiler; maybe the rest was completed when it returned home to 16A. We are at St Pancras terminus and the 7P has arrived with what was probably an express from Nottingham (Midland). Perhaps the time shown by the clock will help any timetable aficionado approximate the working which brought the engine to London. No.45532 transferred from Nottingham to Saltley in June 1961, the production 'Peaks' having taken over many of the express workings from Nottingham (Midland). After almost a year at Saltley, followed by a couple of months at Derby, **ILLUSTRIOUS** returned to the WCML at Upperby where it would end its days in 1964.

Just south of Wigan, No.45533 works homeward bound with a Down fitted freight circa 1959. Now equipped with ATC, the Upperby 6P would remain attached to WCML depots for the rest of its life. After its time at Upperby, **LORD RATHMORE** transferred to Rugby in November 1959 then, just over a year later it was sent to Nuneaton of all places – it wasn't alone, at least five others joined it there – but some dignity was regained in September 1961 with a final move to Edge Hill for its last year. *Book Law Publications.*

Perhaps it was all fitted freights from 12B. Here is No.45533 on Shap circa 1959.

Note how some nameplates spread the lettering whilst others squeeze them in. When was this plate made and when was it fitted to the engine?

No.45534 **E.TOOTAL BROADHURST** runs past the southern throat of Basford Hall yard on the Up fast on 10th June 1956. An Edge Hill engine during much of the Fifties' decade, we can assume that the express started from Liverpool. The day when this image was captured on film was a Sunday hence the rather deserted tracks leading to and from the marshalling yard; during weekdays from this vantage point on the Casey overbridge, you would see two or more trains in transit entering or leaving the yard. Locomotives attending works from the south would normally enter Crewe via this route.

No.45534 four years later, in July 1960, whilst working a Manchester (London Road)–London (Euston) morning express and taking the Crewe line through Cheadle Hulme. A few detail changes have been collected over the intervening years; ATC has been fitted and the new BR crest now adorns the tender sides. Note, however, that electrification warning flashes are yet to be fitted. Allocated to 9A from 18th June to 10th September 1960, the 7P was sent to Longsight to cover for a motive power shortage at the depot during the turmoil of the changes being brought about on the main line into London Road station.

Another 'tight' nameplate where even the fixing holes compete for space!

No.45535 **SIR HERBERT WALKER K.C.B.** works a Down express. We are at Lichfield T.V. on an unrecorded date but it is pre-ATC ands the engine wears an 8A shed plate which would put the date between 1954 and near to the end of that decade – apologies for not being more specific. The ex-works WD is no help as its number is slightly out of focus. Long before rebuilding of certain members of the class was even contemplated, this engine spent some years working from Holbeck – from new to February 1935, and July 1936 to August 1948 – along with sisters 5534 and 5538. However, none of them returned to Leeds; Derby built No.5534 was rebuilt, whilst Crewe built No.5538 was not rebuilt! It might be worth listing here the various depots to which the class was allocated to during their lifetime: Annesley, Aston, Bank Hall, Bescot, Blackpool, Bristol Barrow Road, Bushbury, Camden, Carnforth, Crewe North, Darnall, Derby, Edge Hill, Holbeck, Holyhead, Kentish Town, Kingmoor, Lancaster, Llandudno Junction, Longsight, Mold Junction, Newton Heath, Northwich, Nottingham, Nuneaton, Patricroft, Polmadie, Preston, Rugby, Saltley, Shrewsbury, Springs Branch, Trafford Park, Upperby, Warrington, Willesden – 37 in all!

Why use two lines when it all fits in one – just!

Heading south through Longsight with a London train circa 1955, No.45536 **PRIVATE W.WOOD, V.C.** looks hardly fit for purpose on this gloriously sunny afternoon. Except for a few years at the likes of Preston, Crewe North, Upperby and Bushbury, this 7P had spent much of its life allocated to 9A. During the whole of the 1950s it was resident at the Manchester shed which was appropriate because of the depot's connection with the Victoria Cross winner (Wilf Wood was a Running Foreman at Longsight until retirement in 1960). He named No.5536 in his own honour during 1936 when the class was still known as the 'Baby Scots.' For those who know nothing of Wilf Wood's military exploits, it is worth mentioning that he was a Private in the 10th Battalion, Northumberland Fusiliers (he was born – 1897 – and raised in Stockport and worked at Edgeley shed up to enlisting. Why the Northumberland Fusiliers? I don't know but he started military life in 1916 as a stretcher bearer with the Cheshire Regiment before transferring). He won his V.C. during an action near Casa Vana in Italy on 28th October 1918 when he took an enemy machine gun position, and caused 140 men to surrender. He later repeated the exploit when he took a German held position and some 163 enemy surrendered. He died peacefully at home in Hazel Grove during January 1982.

The great man's plate when it was attached to No.45536. Luckily one of the nameplates was presented to the Northumberland Fusiliers Regimental museum at Alnwick where it is held in more reverence than it was in BR days.

With the coming of the diesels and electrics, life for steam was difficult at Longsight although some managed to stick around the place until the mid 1960s. No.45536 was not one of the latter and was transferred to Sheffield Darnall, along with other 7Ps, where it was less than welcome. In store since April 1962 at Staveley GC shed – Darnall shed did not require its services so the alternative was redundancy – No.45536 was condemned in December 1962 and was eventually taken to Crewe for cutting-up in 1964. *Book Law Publications.*

This has got to be the summer of 61' when contractors had taken over Stafford station and passengers' requirements were basically ignored. It would be interesting to arrange a similar scenario nowadays and then invite the H&SE to comment/act! Nuneaton's No.45538 **GIGGLESWICK** has just arrived with a Down working which would hardly have kept it in check but it was work. 2B kept this engine going until September 1962 when Crewe called and the 6P went north for the last time.

A nice rear three-quarter view of No.45539 **E.C.TRENCH** calling at Lancaster with a Down working on an unrecorded date, probably in the mid to late Fifties' when the 6P was allocated to Edge Hill.

The nameplate when fitted to the engine.

Whilst Stafford station was in the throes of rebuilding in the early Sixties' No.45540 **SIR ROBERT TURNBULL** calls with an Up express. The 7P is wearing a 12B shedplate which puts our illustration as post July 1962 which ties in nicely however, look at the BR emblem on the tender (No.9758); did the tender ever receive the BR crest? The early April 1963 withdrawal of SIR BOB would indicate a negative! Although some electrification catenary has been erected at the north end of the platforms, there is little sign of wires at this end of the station yet but note the water column between the Up fast and slow lines – just in case, but not for much longer!

No.45541 **DUKE OF SUTHERLAND** stopped at Tamworth (Low Level) with what appears to be a horse-box special. This engine was allocated to Rugby for the twelve months from November 1959 until it transferred down the road to nearby Nuneaton in December 1960. Views of 'Patriots' with 2A shed plates in BR days are extremely rare; well they would be wouldn't they?

The only Duke on the LMS.

An undated view of Upperby's No.45542 working through Droylsden in east Manchester with a trans-Pennine express circa 1956.

Sunday rest in Scotland! Preston's un-named No.45542 stabled on Polmadie shed yard in May 1959. *D.H.Beecroft.*

Fore and aft views of No.45542 undergoing overhaul at Crewe in March 1960. The tenderless 'Patriot' appears to have 'Jubilee' No.45591 **UDIAPUR** for company. At the top right corner of the cabside plate can be seen the remains of a long elapsed experiment which BR began in the early Fifties' but did not pursue after adverse reactions from footplatemen. The long bracket was supposed to hold a plate with the name of the driver printed thereon. All regions tried to start it but none were successful in getting the men to accept the scheme. *both D.H.Beecroft.*

Outside the roundhouse, No.45543 **HOME GUARD** is being prepared for an afternoon working at Upperby circa 1955.

Some years later and No.45543 is on rail tour duty. The date is 14th December 1962 and the venue is Derby shed where the by-now Carnforth based 6P is ready to work the *LCGB THE MIDLAND LIMITED RAILTOUR*. Although not spotless, the engine has had a complimentary 'rub over' and the name has been cleaned. ATC and electrification warning flashes are now the 'order of the day' for the WCML based members of the class. However, this engine had been withdrawn a month beforehand during week ending 17th November 1962 so why was it brought out of retirement for this event? The big bad winter had yet to get going so not many, if any, of the resurrected steam locomotives were yet to be fired-up. So what is the story behind this resurrection?

Making it look easy on Shap. No.45544 at Scout Green with just eight on!

Upperby's No.45544 was a visitor to Polmadie on 3rd December 1959. Most 'Patriots' were visitors to 66A as few of the class were ever allocated, none as 7P rebuilds. Those that were included: 5528 - 11th May 1935 to 28th December 1940; 5549 - new to 18th January 1941; 5550 - 6th July 1934 to 7th December 1940. All, it will be noted, leaving during the second winter of the war.

No.45545 **PLANET** at Newton Heath shed on a glorious summer afternoon circa 1960.

The nameplate when the engine was looking a bit more presentable, probably in 1948.

Unaided, No.45546 **FLEETWOOD** climbs through Shap Wells in the 1950s with a considerable load of thirteen vehicles. Pure speculation – it was there for much of the latter half of the decade – would put the engine as allocated to Crewe North. Off the scale of 'normal' depots associated with the class, Carnforth, Mold Junction, and Warrington were its last sheds.

(above) A late evening sun highlights the flanks of No.45547 at Crewe North shed circa 1954. *K.R.Pirt. (below)* About four years later, and No.45547 is allocated to Willesden but has worked to Stafford on this occasion where another evening foray by one of our photographers has captured the right side of the engine once again. Note the newly-applied but wrong-facing crest!

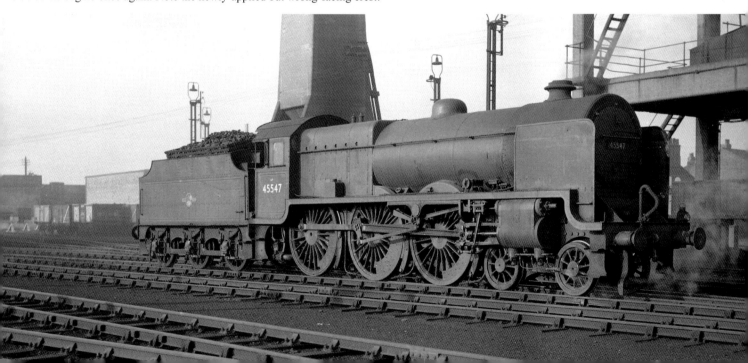

No.45547 double-heads 'Princess Royal' No.46212 **DUCHESS OF KENT** out of Citadel station Carlisle with *THE MID-DAY SCOT* on Thursday 12th August 1954. The Crewe North 'Patriot' may well have been simply hitching a lift home but I would like to think that the load was regarded as a little heavy, even for a Pacific.

Some years later and No.45547 has sole charge of an Up WCML express during the days when the line was being prepared for electrification. Now serving Edge Hill shed, the 6P has gained ATC, and the electrification warning flashes. 8A was its last shed and it was from there that withdrawal took place in September 1962. The bridge carried the A38 Trunk road at the time and in order to get the required clearance for the overhead catenary, new concrete arches were being cast on top of the original masonry arches. Once the concrete was sufficiently cured, the old arch was usually removed by explosive charges in a somewhat spectacular but totally controlled explosion. This method was employed up and down the main line and, as far as is known, the result each time was a total success!

Another Crewe North 'Patriot' stables on Newton Heath shed at sometime in the Fifties' (45548 transferred to Carnforth 7th November 1959). No.45548 **LYTHAM ST.ANNES**, along with No.5547, was allocated to Newton Heath shortly after coming into service in 1934. Both engines resided until the middle years of WW2 – 5547 transferred to Crewe North in December 1942 and our subject followed a month later. It was whilst working from the Manchester depot that the name was bestowed on No.5548 in 1937, highly appropriate in the circumstances as both of the then 5Xs were regular visitors to the Fylde coast. For the record, No.5546 was also a Newton Heath resident by 1935 – in time for it's naming to **FLEETWOOD**; like the other two it went to Crewe during those dark days of the war. The dark days of June 1962 saw our subject going for scrap.

The nameplate which never had a civic badge or coat of arms.

(above) Not the most technically accomplished of images but nevertheless interesting enough to include within the illustrations presented in this album. No.45549 is stabled on the shed yard at Peterborough Spital Bridge, the former Midland roundhouse located alongside the ECML. We have no date and very few clues as to when this event took place. The 6P was allocated to depots adjacent to or nearby the WCML for all of the 1950s, and it took up residency of its last depot Warrington Dallam in April 1960. ATC is not fitted and the tender seems to sport an original pre-1957 BR emblem. Spital Bridge closed on 1st February 1960! This was one of half a dozen of the class which managed to remain coupled to the same tender throughout their lives; the others were Nos.45504 (4476), 45506 (4478), 45509 (4481), 45519 (4491), and 45548 (4555); 45549 was coupled to No.4556. *(below)* No.45549 seemed to have a prevalence for roaming, but not necessarily to exotic places. This is the 6P heading out of Whitley Bay on the evening of Friday 24th May 1957 with what appears to be an excursion from the LMR. At the time No.45549 was an Upperby engine, and working over from Carlisle via the N&C line with a train load of day-trippers wanting to sample the delights of the east coast resort, would be easy for the 6P. Coast-to-coast! *Both Book Law Publications.*

Upperby's No.5550 climbs away from Tebay in the summer of 1949 whilst working a Down freight. Renumbering of this engine took place in October 1949. No.5550 had transferred to the Carlisle shed in July 1946 after four years at Patricroft where it worked with No.5528, 5542 and 5543 through the War years (5501 and 5529 joined them for four months only in 1942, 5503 for six months in 1941/42). No.5524 actually went new in March 1933 and worked from the west Manchester shed until transferred to Camden in January 1936; it was the only one to do so. Note the high straight-sided tender (No.4573) which was coupled to No.45550 from 29th December 1942 to 23rd January 1956. This was one of the un-named group in this class to which names had been designated by 1943 but had never carried them. No.45550 should have been SIR HENRY FOWLER.

All coaled up and nowhere to go! Although this looks like the driver knows differently. No.45551 at the north end of Kingmoor yard on Sunday 25th May 1952! The 12A shed plate denotes Upperby shed, Kingmoor at this time was in the Scottish Region as 68A. Nevertheless, co-operation between the two depots was excellent through BR days and was a throwback to LMS days. Of course, in 1958 Kingmoor 'moved' to the LM Region and became 12A with Upperby becoming 12B. Shed plates were exchanged, new ones acquired and all sorts of paperwork changed hands. The locomotives remained virtually status quo with lending being the order of the day, just like before!

Except for fourteen days spent at Crewe North shed in January 1950, No.45551 spent the whole of the 1950s as a resident of Upperby shed (right up to 25th June 1960) and here she is about mid-way through that tenure at the head of a southbound express early on a summers' afternoon. Making a dramatic getaway from Citadel station, the 6P looks fairly clean, if not quite resplendent. Only fifteen of the class never served Upperby shed, the others, accumulatively, always had a presence at the depot throughout the life of the class.